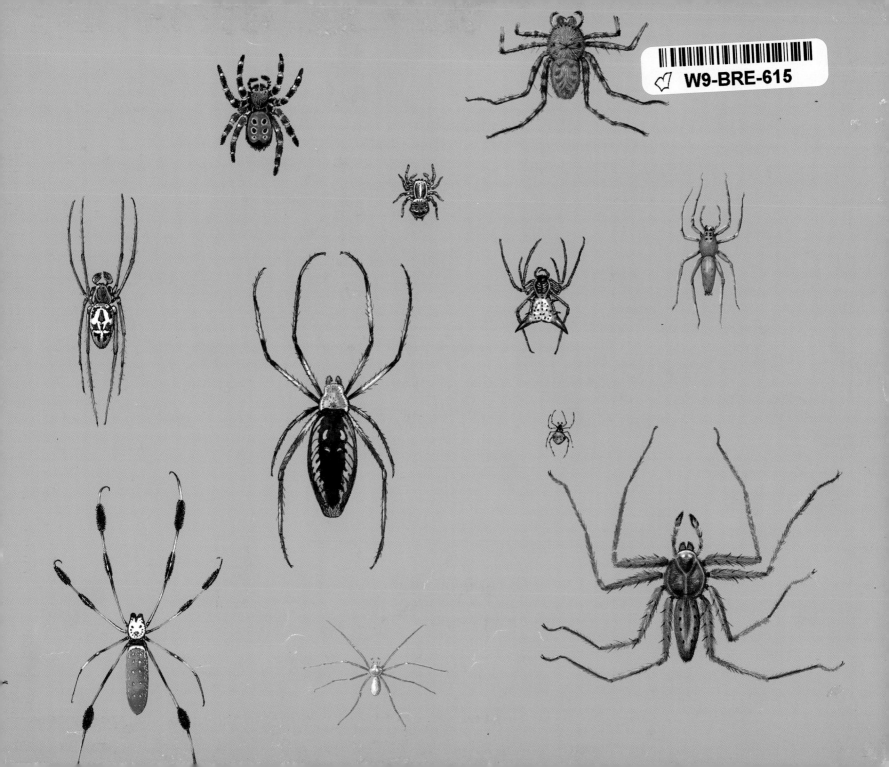

LET'S-READ-AND-FIND-OUT SCIENCE®

STAGE 2

Spinning Spiders

by Melvin Berger • illustrated by S. D. Schindler

HarperCollins*Publishers*

For Ben Mueller from his Zayde,
with much love
—M.B.

Special thanks to Dr. Stanley Green
of Penn State University
for his time and expert review

The *Let's-Read-and-Find-Out Science* book series was originated by Dr. Franklyn M. Branley, Astronomer Emeritus and former Chairman of the American Museum–Hayden Planetarium, and was formerly co-edited by him and Dr. Roma Gans, Professor Emeritus of Childhood Education, Teachers College, Columbia University. Text and illustrations for each of the books in the series are checked for accuracy by an expert in the relevant field. For more information about Let's-Read-and-Find-Out Science books, write to HarperCollins Children's Books, 1350 Avenue of the Americas, New York, NY 10019, or visit our website at www.letsreadandfindout.com.

HarperCollins®, ☀®, and Let's Read-and-Find-Out Science® are trademarks of HarperCollins Publishers Inc.

Library of Congress Cataloging-in-Publication Data
Berger, Melvin.
Spinning spiders / by Melvin Berger ; illustrated by S.D. Schindler.
p.   cm. — (Let's-read-and-find-out science. Stage 2)
Summary: Describes the characteristics of spiders and the methods they use to trap their prey in webs.
ISBN 0-06-028696-2 — ISBN 0-06-445207-7 (pbk.) —ISBN 0-06-028697-0 (lib. bdg.)
1. Spiders—Juvenile literature. [1. Spiders.] I. Schindler, S.D., ill. II. Title. III. Series.
QL458.4 .B473 2003
595.4'4—dc21
2001039507
CIP
AC

Typography by Elynn Cohen
4 5 6 7 8 9 10 ❖ First Edition

Spinning Spiders

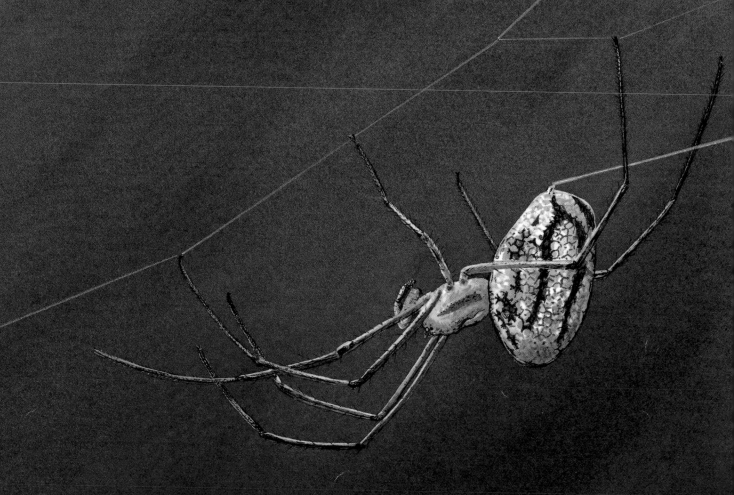

Spiderwebs are everywhere. You find them high up on walls and windows, on lamps and lights, in dark corners. Sheds, barns, and garages are favorite places for spiderwebs. Outdoors you find them on trees and plants, on swings and slides, on poles and fences, and even in the grass.

New spiderwebs are beautiful patterns of thin threads. Old webs may be covered with dirt and dust. We call them cobwebs.

There are more than thirty thousand kinds of spiders. They can be small or large, fat or thin, short or long. Most are brown, gray, black, or other dull colors. But a few are as bright and colorful as flowers.

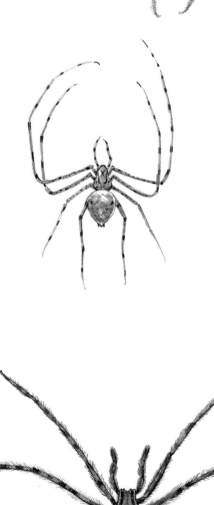

Most people confuse spiders and insects. Spiders are *not* insects. Spiders are arachnids (uh-RAK-nids). Some other well-known arachnids are mites, ticks, and scorpions.

Arachnids differ from insects in a few ways.

Arachnids have eight legs.
Insects have six legs.

Adult arachnids have no wings.
Most adult insects have wings.

Arachnid bodies have two main parts.
Insect bodies have three main parts.

Arachnids have no feelers or antennae.
Insects have antennae.

9

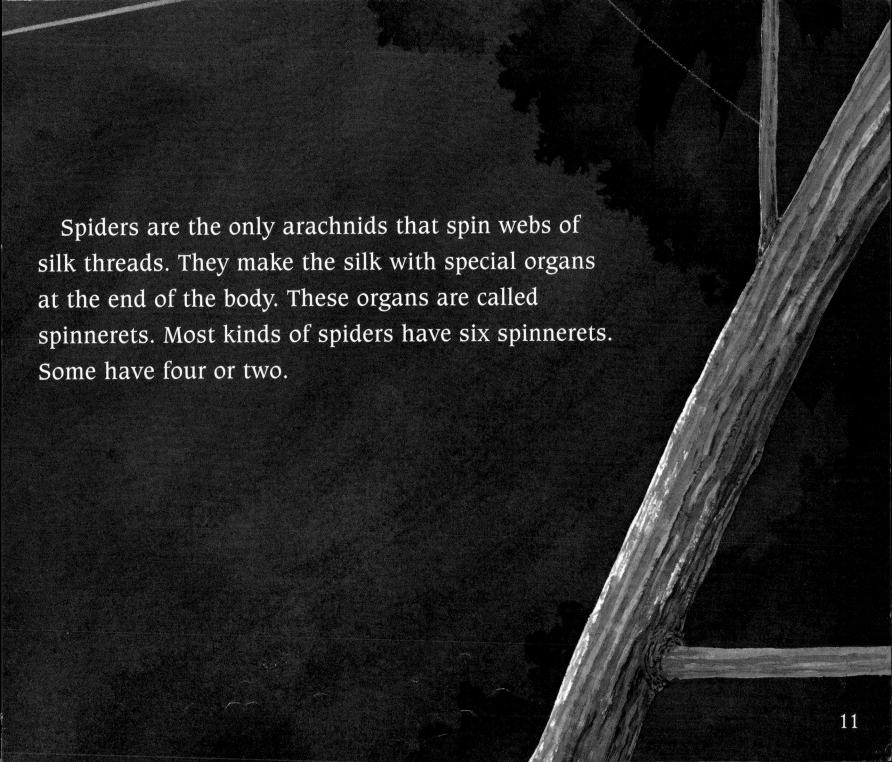

Spiders are the only arachnids that spin webs of silk threads. They make the silk with special organs at the end of the body. These organs are called spinnerets. Most kinds of spiders have six spinnerets. Some have four or two.

A liquid comes out of the spinnerets. Outside the body, the liquid hardens into a solid thread of silk. The thread is very thin. But it is very sticky. It is also stronger than a steel thread that size, and it can stretch. The silk thread can stretch to almost twice its length!

Many spiders use the silk to make webs. The webs are to catch the insects they eat.

If a fly buzzes too close to a spiderweb, it gets caught
on the sticky threads. The fly tries to pull away. It flaps
its wings. It kicks its feet. It wiggles and wriggles. But it
cannot escape. It is stuck in the web's threads.

Most spiders grab the fly with their two fangs. They wrap the fly's body with silk so that it cannot move. Then they inject a poison into the fly.

The poison dissolves the inside of the fly's body.
Spiders don't have teeth. They can't chew. They can only
drink. Once the fly's insides have turned to mush, the
spider can slurp it up. A spider usually eats about one
bug a week, and sometimes more.

The web helps the spider to get the food it needs. The web also protects the spider from its enemies. If an enemy touches the web, the spider feels it. It runs away to safety.

Snakes, frogs, birds, and lizards love to eat spiders. So do wasps and other spiders.

Spiderwebs come in all sizes and shapes. The webs may be neat or jumbled, flat or bowl-shaped, triangular or round. Each kind of web is different.

The web of the common house spider is called a tangled web. The spider attaches long, loose threads

to a wall or window,
a ceiling or corner,
the bottom of a table or chair.

Then the spider joins the thread together with more threads going in every direction.

21

The grass spider usually spins a funnel web in tall grass or low bushes. It looks like a short, wide ice-cream cone. The grass spider hides at the bottom of the cone. When an insect lands on the top part, the grass spider dashes up and grabs its meal.

The platform spider weaves flat sheet webs in trees or
shrubs. It spins separate threads above the sheet web.
If a flying insect hits one of these threads, it falls into
the sheet.

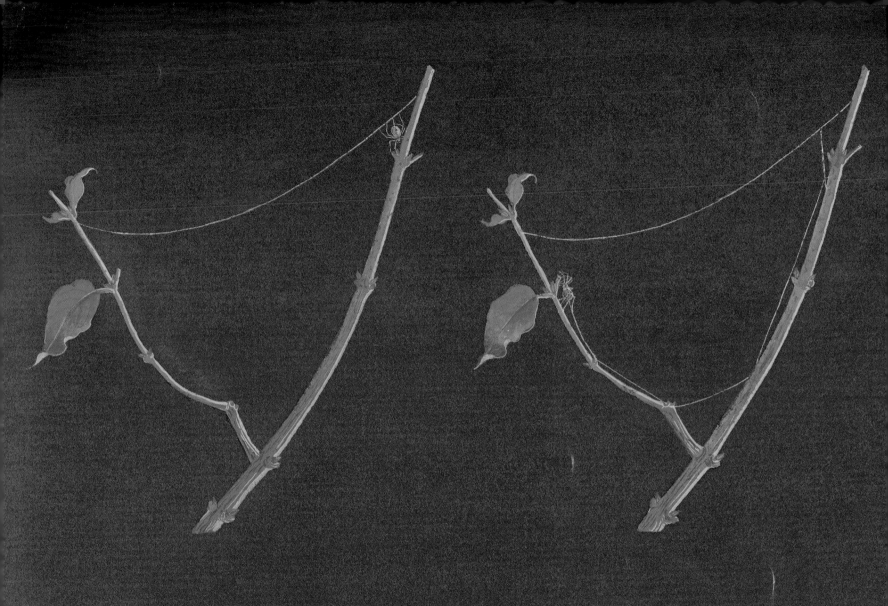

The garden spider builds orb webs on tall grass or flowers. First it weaves a strong thread on which to hang the web. Next, it spins the outside threads of the web.

Then it adds threads that go out from the center like
the spokes of a wheel. Finally, the spider connects the
spokes with coils of sticky silk.

The ogre-faced spider carries its web with it. It hangs from a branch holding the web in its four front legs. When an insect comes near, the ogre-faced spider catches it in the web.

Not all spiders make webs. The
bolas spider spins a thread of silk
with a sticky silk ball at the end.

The spider swings the line at an
insect. The insect gets stuck on
the sticky ball of thread.

27

The biggest spider of all doesn't need a web to catch its prey. The tarantula can be up to ten inches across. That's as wide as a dinner plate! Because they are so large, tarantulas usually eat small birds, snakes, mice, frogs, and even fish, as well as insects. Tarantulas can live for about twenty years.

Altogether, spiders eat *millions* of insects every day of the year. Many of these insects can harm or annoy people. In this way, spiders help us live better.

Spiders are also food for many different birds, fish, and frogs. So if you see a spider, let it be. Spiders are an important part of life on earth.

What's So Scary?

Many people have the wrong idea about spiders. They think that all spiders are dangerous. In fact, the fear of spiders is very common.

Most spiders, though, don't hurt people. A spider's bite may stun or kill an insect or a small animal, but spiders rarely injure human beings.

In the United States, only two kinds of spiders can bite you. They are the widow spiders (including the black widow) and the brown recluse spider. Both kinds are very shy. They usually run away if you get close. So there's no reason to be scared of spiders!

BROWN RECLUSE SPIDER

BLACK WIDOW SPIDER

A Web of Your Own

You may like to have a pretty spiderweb to hang on your wall. You can get one without harming a spider. You will need:

- talcum powder
- a sheet of construction paper (black or another dark color)
- spray adhesive (you can buy this at most art-supply stores)

1. Go outdoors on a warm day. Look for a nice, neat web around a plant or bush or around a door or window. Make sure there is no spider on the web!
2. When you find a web, gently sprinkle it with talcum powder. Then use two hands to hold the construction paper flat behind the web. Slowly and carefully lift the paper so that the web sticks to it. The spider won't mind. Spiders often spin new webs every day.
3. Hold the spray adhesive can about eight inches from the paper and spray the web. Set the paper down to dry. Soon the web will be ready to hang on your wall. Enjoy its beautiful shape and design.

You can find out more about spiders at these websites:

http://atshq.org (official website of The American Tarantula Society)
http://www.insects.org (excellent site with information on spiders and insects)